MAHESH MATHPAL

Money Matters: For Young Minds

Copyright © 2024 by MAHESH MATHPAL

All rights reserved. No part of this publication may be reproduced, stored or transmitted in any form or by any means, electronic, mechanical, photocopying, recording, scanning, or otherwise without written permission from the publisher. It is illegal to copy this book, post it to a website, or distribute it by any other means without permission.

First edition

*This book was professionally typeset on Reedsy.
Find out more at reedsy.com*

Dedicated to the dreamers, the future leaders, and the savvy thinkers of tomorrow—may you always count more than just dollars and know that true wealth is built with wisdom, not just wallet. To the young minds who dare to dream big, think smart, and see the world beyond the numbers—may you master the art of money while never losing sight of what truly makes you rich.

"Money is a tool. Used properly, it makes something beautiful; used wrong, it makes a mess."
— Bradley Vinson

Contents

Foreword — iii
Preface — vi
Acknowledgments — viii

1. Introduction — 1
2. Money—It's More Than Just Paper — 5
3. From Barter To Banknotes—The Evolution of Money — 9
4. Money vs. Currency—What's the Real Deal? — 14
5. The Rise of the Dollar—How It Became the World's Reserve... — 19
6. The Gold Standard—A Golden Era for Money? — 24
7. The End of the Gold Standard and the Rise of Fiat Money — 29
8. The Rise of Digital Money and the Role of Banks — 33
9. The Crypto Revolution: Challenging Traditional Money — 38
10. Chapter 10 — 42
11. The Shift Away from the U.S. Dollar – A Changing Global... — 45
12. Mastering Money in a Choppy World – Your Guide to Financial... — 49
13. Money, Price, Inflation, Banks, and You – How Money and... — 55

| 14 | Conclusion– Young Minds Embracing a New Financial World | 58 |

About the Author 62
Also by MAHESH MATHPAL 63

Foreword

Why This Book Will Change the Way You Think About Money

Let's be honest—most books about money aren't exactly thrilling, especially if you're young. Their language is dry, the examples are outdated, and by the time you reach the end of the first chapter, you're left wondering: How does any of this apply to me? But *Money Matters for Young Minds* is different, and I'm here to tell you why.

You're probably already using money in some form every day. Maybe you're saving for the latest tech gadget, paying for an online subscription, or eyeing a new pair of sneakers. But how much do you really know about money? How does it work? Where did it come from? And most importantly—how can understanding it better help you in your life?

This book takes what many would consider a "boring" subject and makes it digestible and exciting (yes, even fun). It's packed with real-life examples, stories, and even a few witty metaphors to help you wrap your head around some pretty complex topics. And, unlike other books, it's written specifically for you—the young minds, already part of today's fast-evolving financial world, whether you realize it or not.

Why buy and read This Book?

If you've ever thought that financial literacy was just something adults worry about, think again. The financial world is changing rapidly, and you're smack in the middle. Whether digital payments, cryptocurrencies, or even the rise of things like NFTs, how we think about and use money is evolving, and it's doing so faster than ever. By reading this book, you're staying ahead of the curve.

But beyond the big-picture stuff, this book is your practical guide to navigating money in your everyday life. It breaks down confusing terms and explains things like budgeting, saving, and even how to make intelligent choices when it comes to borrowing or investing money—all in a way that doesn't feel like a lecture.

Think of it as your financial toolkit, offering strategies that will serve you well for years to come, from high school all the way to your first paycheck(yes, you must start saving right from your first paycheque if you are not saving already) and beyond.

What You'll Miss Without It

Still not convinced? Let me give you a glimpse of what you'll miss if you don't dive into these pages. First, you might never really grasp the difference between money and currency—and trust me, that's a game-changer. You'll miss out on understanding why your $20 bill has no intrinsic value and how things like TRUST and belief play considerable roles in the value of what's in your wallet.

You'll also miss out on some of the most remarkable stories about the evolution of money. How did we go from trading goats to using invisible, digital coins? Why is the U.S. dollar such a big deal in global trade? And what's the deal with cryptocurrencies, anyway? These are questions you'll get answered and explained in a way that makes sense for the world you're living in today.

In Short: Don't Skip This

By the end of this book, you won't just understand how money works—you'll know 'how it works for you.' And trust me, that's the kind of knowledge that can change your life. So flip to Chapter 1 and get ready to explore a subject that's way more exciting than you ever thought possible.

A good book is one that not only teaches you something but also encourages you to learn more about the subject matter. This book provides enough material to grasp the essence of money and kindle your desire to learn more about it. I am sure young minds reading this book are bubbling with ideas to be implemented and benefit immensely.

Your future self—and your future bank account—will thank you!

Preface

Navigating the New Financial Frontier

Welcome to **Money Matters: For Young Minds**. This book has been crafted with a clear purpose: to demystify the world of money for teenagers and young adults. In a time when financial literacy is more crucial than ever, understanding money's role in our lives is beneficial and essential.

In an ever-evolving economic landscape, young minds are often left out of conversations about financial principles, emerging technologies, and global economic shifts. This book fills that gap by offering an engaging, accessible introduction to the intricacies of money and its various forms. From the historical evolution of money and the concept of fiat currencies to the rise of digital assets like cryptocurrencies, we aim to provide a comprehensive foundation to serve you well throughout your financial journey.

Each chapter is designed to break down complex concepts into digestible, relatable information. We explore not only the basics—like what money is and how it functions—but also delve into how modern financial systems work, including the role of banks, the significance of the dollar, and the impact of emerging technologies on global economies.

We aim to empower you with knowledge to help you make informed financial decisions, whether saving for your first big purchase, planning for college, or simply trying to understand how the economy affects you. By the end of this book, you'll not only grasp the essentials of money management but also gain insights into the future of finance.

As you turn these pages, remember that understanding money is not just about numbers—it's about understanding your potential and preparing for a world where financial literacy is a key to success.

Enjoy the journey, and let's embark on this financial adventure together!

Acknowledgments

The author draws inspiration from the content available on open internet platforms while writing the book.

Different authorities have opinions on various issues, which sometimes vary from those of others. Young minds must respect these differences and try to grasp the best out of everything available to them,

1

Introduction

Why Money Matters More Than You Think

Let's face it—money is woven into every aspect of your life. It's in your morning coffee, your favorite sneakers, and even that streaming service you binge on. But have you ever stopped to think about what money is?

Sure, you probably know it buys stuff, but money is more than just the dollar bills (or the numbers on your banking app). It's a tool that influences nearly every decision you make, whether you know it or not. And yet, for something so essential, it's wild how little time we spend learning about it.

Most teens know more about the latest 'Instagram' trend than they do about money management—and that's not their fault. Financial literacy isn't exactly a school subject, but it should be! Trust me; the impact of understanding (or not understanding) how money works is enormous(and can sometimes be devastating).

Why You Should Care About Money

Let's break it down: money doesn't just shape what's in your closet or what's on your dinner table. It determines bigger things, like your career path, where you live, and even when (or if) you can retire someday. But the story of money isn't just about adults dealing with mortgages and retirement accounts—the decisions you make 'right now' as a teenager set the stage for your financial future.

Are you saving up for an iPhone? Figuring out how to afford college? That's the start of your money journey. And here's the kicker: knowing how to handle money early on gives you a massive head start on the rest of your life.

It's like getting the cheat codes for a game, but the stakes are much higher.

The Problem: No One Talks About This Stuff!

Now, the big question: why aren't more people talking about money? The truth is, the world of finance can seem intimidating. Words like "inflation" and "compound interest" can sound like they belong in a classroom lecture, and who wants that?

Most of the time, adults are too busy or shy to talk about money straightforwardly. It's almost like there's a secret club for people who "get" how money works, and if you're not in it, well…good luck figuring it out on your own.

But here's the good news: that's precisely what this book is for! We're pulling back the curtain, laying it all out so you don't have to guess. You might not be worried about mortgages or loans right now, but the same principles apply to minor decisions like credit cards, saving, and investing. Knowing how to handle money means avoiding the financial traps that could cause significant problems down the road.

So...What Is Money, Really?

Before we dive too deep into the hows and whys, let's tackle the basics:

What even is money?

At its simplest, money is a tool that lets people trade things easily. Imagine living in a world where you had to barter—a pair of shoes for a sandwich or a phone charger for a ride to school. It'd be messy, right?

Money simplifies all of that by giving everyone a common language for exchange. Whether it's in the form of cash, coins, or digital currency, it's just a way to measure and store value.

But don't be fooled by its simplicity. Money has become a powerful force, shaping entire economies, nations, and history.

Case in Point: A Financial Disaster in the Making

Need some real-life examples of why financial knowledge matters? Take the 2008 financial crisis. Back then, millions lost their jobs and homes because they, and even some banks, didn't fully understand how money worked—specifically, loans and credit. Entire families were thrown into chaos, *all because they hadn't been taught how to manage their money effectively.*

The Goal: Empowering You with Financial Smarts

Here's where we come in. *Money Matters: For Young Minds* aims to give you the tools to understand the 'what,' 'why,' and 'how' of money. We're not just talking about essential saving tips—though those are important too—but about building a deeper understanding of how money functions worldwide.

You'll learn here things like:

- How money came to be: Spoiler alert—it wasn't always about paper bills and coins.

- Why some people struggle with money, and others seem to have plenty: Hint: it's not always about how much they earn.

- How money affects your decisions and your choices as you grow up.

This knowledge will give you the confidence to make better choices—whether you're trying to afford that next concert ticket or planning for something bigger, like college.

Why It's More Than Just Dollars and Cents

Understanding money isn't just about becoming rich (although that's nice, too!). It's about freedom—the freedom to make choices, take risks, and shape your future. When you know how to manage money, you're in control. You get to decide what's important and how you will make it happen.

So, whether you're saving for your first car or figuring out how to budget your summer job paycheck, consider this book your crash course in everything you need to know.

Because money matters—a lot more than you might think. And with some know-how, you'll be able to master it. Ready to start your financial journey?

Let's dive in!

2

Money—It's More Than Just Paper

Let's be honest: when someone says 'money,' you probably think of crumpled notes, shiny coins, or even a number on your phone's banking app. But money, as simple as it seems, is one of the most brilliant inventions humanity has ever come up with. It's the silent hero in every transaction we make—whether it's grabbing a snack at school or streaming your favourite playlist.

But what is money, really? Is it just those green slips of paper? Nope! Money is way more than that. It's a concept, a tool that humans created to make life a lot easier. It also has three essential functions that keep the entire system of trade and economics ticking along like a well-oiled machine.

Function 1: Medium of Exchange

Imagine this: You've got a goat but need a pair of shoes. The local shoemaker, however, has no interest in your goat because he's more of a cat person. Economists call this the 'double coincidence of wants,' which makes bartering annoying. Trading goods directly was a massive hassle, and the world needed a solution that was, well, less…goat-based.

Enter money. Money makes trade simple and efficient. Instead of trying to find someone who wants your goat and has shoes your size, you can sell your goat for money. Then, you can use that money to buy those perfect sneakers from the shoemaker who never cared about your goat in the first place.

Money is this magical medium that allows everyone to trade quickly without needing to *match their wants* exactly. In short, it's like the universal translator of trade—everyone speaks its language.

Function 2: Store of Value

The second superpower of money is its ability to 'store value over time.' This is a big one. Imagine if you couldn't save money. Like, say you mowed lawns all summer and got paid in, I don't know, apples. That's great if you're really into apples, but the problem is, they will rot before you can use them to buy anything worthwhile. That is why bartering wasn't just awkward—it was impractical for saving up for anything significant.

Money, on the other hand, doesn't rot. You can earn it, stash it in a savings account, and know that when you're ready, you can use it to buy something later. Whether saving for the next Macbook Pro or putting money away for college, you can trust that your money will hold its value over time (unless inflation kicks in, but we'll get to that fun topic later).

In essence, money is a bit like a time capsule. It allows you to store the work you did yesterday for what you want tomorrow.

Function 3: Unit of Account

Have you ever tried to compare two different things and wondered which is "worth" more? How many cheeseburgers can you get for the price of one video game? Or how does the cost of a pair of shoes stack up against a concert ticket?

That is where money's third function—a unit of account—comes in handy. Money gives us a way to measure the value of different things, making it easy to compare and decide what's worth what. It provides a consistent way to price goods and services (we will discuss price in detail soon), so you don't have to guess or argue about how many fries equal one T-shirt. Think of it as the scoreboard of the economy—it lets us know who's winning, losing, or just breaking even in the great game of commerce.

Money in the Wild: A Quick Case Study

Let's look at how these functions play out in real life—Have you ever heard of the Venezuelan economic crisis? In 2010, hyperinflation (a scary word for prices skyrocketing out of control- we will learn more about hyperinflation soon) caused the Venezuelan currency, the bolívar, to lose value so quickly that people were walking around with wheelbarrows of cash just to buy groceries.

Why? Because the bolívar stopped working as a 'store of value'—money that loses its value fast isn't very useful. People even started using eggs or flour for trade because they held their value better than cash.

That's how essential these three functions of money are. When one breaks down, the whole system falls apart.

Money's Evolution: From Seashells to Bitcoins

Believe it or not, the cash in your wallet isn't the only form of money humans have used. At different times and places, money has been everything from large stones (look up 'Rai stones' if you want a good laugh) to seashells to chunks of gold.

Today, with digital money, cryptocurrencies like Bitcoin are shaking things up again, but they all still rely on those same three essential functions.

So, the next time you pull a dollar out of your pocket, remember—it's more than just paper. It's a tool that makes your life easier, holds your hard-earned value, and helps you determine how many pizzas you can get for your allowance. And understanding how this tool works is the first step to mastering it.

Because if there's one thing you'll learn from this book, it's that money really 'does' matter—more than you think.

3

From Barter To Banknotes—The Evolution of Money

Before credit cards, mobile payments, and paper bills, there was barter—a system where people directly exchanged goods and services. Imagine living in a time when, if you wanted something, you'd have to find someone who had it and enjoyed what 'you' had to offer in return. This system worked, but it was clunky, inefficient, and, quite frankly, a headache. It was clear that humanity needed a more efficient way to facilitate trade than bartering.

Thus began the fascinating evolution of money!

Bartering: The Early Days of Trade

- In the earliest human societies, bartering was the norm. Communities traded everything from food and livestock to tools and clothing. For example, if you were a farmer with extra crops, you might exchange them for tools made by a blacksmith. But, as you can imagine, this system had severe limitations:

- What if the blacksmith already had enough crops and didn't need more?

- What if what you were trading wasn't equal in value to what you wanted to receive?

This constant need to find the perfect trading partner made commerce inefficient and limited the growth of early economies. Something more standardised was necessary, and that's when early humans turned to commodity money.

Commodity Money: Turning Objects Into Value

To solve the problem of bartering, early civilizations began using 'commodity money'—items that had inherent value and could be traded for goods and services. These commodities were usually chosen for their usefulness, durability, and rarity. Some of the most popular items used as commodity money included:

- Shells: Used by many ancient cultures, shells were durable and relatively rare, making them a suitable medium of exchange.
- Salt: Salt was so valuable in places like ancient Rome that soldiers were often paid in it, giving rise to the phrase "worth your salt."
- Precious metals: Gold, silver, and copper were prized for their beauty and rarity. They were also durable, easily divisible, and portable, qualities that made them excellent for trade.

Take, for example, ancient Mesopotamia. Around 3000 BCE, the people of Mesopotamia used barley as a form of commodity money. It was practical because barley had an inherent use—it could be eaten or planted. However, as civilizations expanded, it became clear that using food, shells, or livestock as money wasn't always the most convenient. Imagine trying to carry enough salt to buy a house, or what might happen to your barley savings in a rainy season!

The Birth of Metal Coins: A Revolutionary Leap

Enter the age of metal coins. Around 600 BCE, the ancient Lydians (in what is now Turkey) were among the first to mint metal coins made of gold and silver. These coins had several advantages over commodity money:

- Durability: Unlike barley or shells, metal coins didn't spoil or break easily.
- Portability: Metal coins were more accessible to carry and transport than bags of grain or livestock.
- Standardisation: Coins were stamped with a standard weight and symbol, making their value easily recognizable and universally accepted.

The use of metal coins quickly spread across ancient civilizations. The Greeks and Romans adopted coinage, which became vital to their economies. Coins made trade more accessible and helped governments exert control over their economies by regulating the supply and standard of money.

For instance, coins were made primarily from gold, silver, bronze, etc., during the Roman Empire, and their value was tied to their metal content. Roman emperors often used coinage to fund public projects, pay soldiers, and influence public opinion.

However, when the government started debasing the currency—mixing base metals with silver to create more coins—people lost trust in the value of Roman money, contributing to the empire's eventual economic decline.

The Emergence of Paper Money: A Lighter, Smarter Solution

As economies grew and people engaged in more extensive

and more complex transactions, carrying bags of coins became impractical. The next giant leap in the evolution of money came with the invention of 'paper money.'

Paper money originated in China during the Tang Dynasty (618–907 CE). As the first known user of banknotes, the Chinese found a solution to the logistical challenges of metal coins. Transporting large quantities of coins over long distances was risky and cumbersome, especially for merchants.

To make things easier, merchants and wealthy individuals would deposit their coins with trusted agents or government officials, who would issue them a paper note representing the value of their deposit. These notes could be redeemed for their equivalent value in metal coins or other goods.

This system spread to other parts of the world, and by the 13th century, Marco Polo famously wrote about the widespread use of paper money in the Mongol Empire under Kublai Khan.

Europe, however, needed to adopt this new form of money. It wasn't until the 17th century that paper money began to gain traction in Europe, with countries like Sweden and England printing their first banknotes.

Paper money had several advantages:

- Lightweight and convenient: A banknote was far easier to carry than a heavy bag of coins.

- Backed by trust: Originally, paper money was backed by physical commodities like gold or silver. Each note was a promise to pay a certain amount of precious metal.

From Banknotes to Digital Payments: The Modern Era

In today's world, we've gone even further. While coins and paper money are still used, many transactions are now conducted digitally. From debit cards to mobile payments, money has evolved into something that often doesn't physically exist.

But even in this digital age, money's core functions remain the same: it is a medium of exchange, a store of value, and a unit of account.

The evolution of money—from bartering to coins to banknotes and beyond—has been shaped by the need for more efficient, reliable, and portable forms of value exchange.

As economies and technologies continue to evolve, so will the concept of money, but its fundamental purpose remains unchanged:

Making trade easier and economies more robust!

4

Money vs. Currency—What's the Real Deal?

What's in your pocket right now? Some coins? A dollar bill? Maybe just a credit card or, more likely, nothing at all because you're a modern teenager, and everything you own is probably digital. But whatever it is, have you ever thought about what it really represents? Is that crumpled $5 bill money or something else entirely?

Spoiler alert: it's currency. And yes, there's a difference.
   The terms 'money' and 'currency' get tossed around like they're the same thing, but they aren't.

Understanding the difference is like unlocking a secret level in a video game—it won't just make you sound smart at dinner parties (or on Instagram). In addition, it will help you understand why things like inflation or cryptocurrency matter.

Money: The Big Picture
   So, what exactly is money? Think of money as anything that

people widely accept as payment for goods or services. That's pretty broad, right? It can be physical things, like gold or silver. It can even be digital, like Bitcoin. Throughout history, humans have used all sorts of weird stuff as money—shells, cattle, stones, you name it.

As long as people agree that it has value and can be traded for something else, it's money. For example, in ancient times, people in some parts of the world used cattle for cash.

Picture trying to buy a snack by herding cattle into a convenience store. That's what they used to do—sort of. It's not precisely snack shopping, but you get the idea.

Money is about UTILITY—it's valuable because it allows you to get things you want, and people trust that value. Whether shiny metal or some digital coins floating around the internet, money can be money if it is widely accepted and trusted.

Currency: The Government's Favorite Child

Currency is more specific. While all currency is money, not all money is currency. Confusing? Don't worry, it's easier than it sounds. 'Currency' is a government-issued form of money, like the dollar, euro, or yen. It's the official stuff that the government says, "Here, this is what we'll use for transactions."

Currency is a type of 'fiat money.' What's that?

'Fiat' means 'by decree,' so fiat money is valuable because the government says it is. It has no inherent value (unlike gold, which has uses in jewelry and electronics). A $20 bill is just paper and ink. Its worth comes from the fact that we TRUST the government behind it. We all agree to play along with the system, which gives it power.

But here's the twist: we are unsure whether currency is tied to anything solid, like gold or silver. Its value comes from trust—trust in the government that issues it, trust in the economy, trust that people will accept it tomorrow when you try to buy something.

Case Study: The Collapse of Trust in Zimbabwe

Would you like to see what happens when trust disappears? Let's talk about Zimbabwe in the early 2000s. The government printed so much currency that it lost all meaning. People were literally using wheelbarrows of cash to buy a loaf of bread. At one point, they had a 100 trillion Zimbabwean dollar bill (yes, that's real). The problem was that no one trusted the currency anymore, and without trust, it stopped being as valuable as money.

That brings us to the critical issue with currency:

When a government mismanages its economy or prints too much money, it can lead to inflation or hyperinflation (like in Zimbabwe), where the currency loses value quickly. When that happens, people stop accepting it, and it's back to square one—bartering or finding something else to use as money.

Money and currencies lose their value over a period of time due to the following three factors:

Inflation: The Value Roller Coaster

Remember how we said currency has no intrinsic value? That's what makes it vulnerable to things like inflation. Inflation is when prices increase and the currency's value decreases. Suddenly, that dollar in your pocket buys less than last week. Inflation happens for many reasons, but a significant cause is when too much currency is circulated.

Imagine if everyone in your town had unlimited Monopoly money. Pretty soon, no one would care if you handed them a $500 Monopoly bill for a candy bar because 'everyone' has one. It's worthless.

Inflation at normal levels is a fact of life in most economies. A little inflation is acceptable and even expected—it's why things cost more today than they did 20 years ago. But too much inflation, or hyperinflation, like in Zimbabwe or Venezuela, can cause a full-blown economic crisis.

Hyperinflation: When Prices Go Crazy

It happens when prices go up super fast, way more than usual. Imagine you buy a candy bar for $1 today, but next week, it costs $10, and the week after, it's $100! That's hyperinflation. It usually happens when a country prints too much money, and the value of that money drops. People can't afford basic things, and their savings become worthless.

It can seriously damage the economy, making it hard for families to buy food or gas. Countries like Zimbabwe and Venezuela have faced hyperinflation, which has created chaos for everyone living there.

Negative inflation, also called deflation: When Falling Prices Cause Big Problems

Deflation occurs when prices for things go down instead of up. Sounds great, right? But it can be bad for the economy. Imagine you're thinking of buying a new phone, but you notice prices keep dropping. So you wait, thinking it'll get even cheaper. If everyone does this, people will stop buying stuff, and businesses make less money. They might cut jobs, and the economy slows down.

It also makes it harder for people or companies to pay off their loans because money becomes more valuable, making debt more complicated to handle. So, deflation can cause big problems.

Currency vs. Digital Money: The Crypto Challenge

In recent years, things have gotten even more enjoyable. With the rise of 'cryptocurrencies' like Bitcoin, we now have a form of money that isn't controlled by any government at all. Bitcoin, for example, is a kind of digital money, but it isn't currency because the government does not issue it.

People trust it because of the technology behind it (blockchain), and its value comes from that trust—just like currency, but without government backing.

Cryptocurrencies challenge the traditional idea of what currency is. Will governments start issuing their own digital currencies? We'll cover that later in the book, but it's enough to know that the lines between money and currency are getting blurrier by the day.

So, what's the takeaway?

Money can be just about anything that people accept for trade. Conversely, the currency is government-backed, paper or digital, and it works because we all agree it does. But it's that agreement, that trust, which makes all the difference.

5

The Rise of the Dollar—How It Became the World's Reserve Currency

Today, the U.S. dollar is more than just the currency used within the United States. It plays a central role in the global economy, serving as the 'world's reserve currency'—the currency that countries rely on for international trade, savings, and financial stability. But how did the dollar reach this status, and why does it continue to dominate global finance?

The answer lies in history, particularly the aftermath of World War II and a crucial moment in 1944 that forever changed the financial landscape: the 'Bretton Woods Agreement.'

The Global Economy After World War II

The devastation of World War II left much of Europe and Asia in economic ruins. The war had shattered the global financial system, and countries were desperate for a solution to rebuild their economies and prevent future financial crises. The world needed stability, and this is where the United States, with its largely intact economy, stepped in.

By 1944, the U.S. was emerging as the dominant global economic power. Its industrial capacity had grown enormously during the war, and the U.S. held the largest reserves of gold in the world, which had long been a standard for measuring the value of currencies. In this post-war environment, the world looked to the U.S. for leadership in rebuilding the global economy.

The Bretton Woods Agreement: A New Financial System

In July 1944, representatives from 44 nations met in Bretton Woods, New Hampshire, to create a new international financial system to promote stability and facilitate global trade. The result was the 'Bretton Woods Agreement,' a landmark decision that shaped the global economy for decades to come. Under this agreement, the U.S. dollar became the central currency in the international financial system. Here's how it worked:

- The U.S. dollar was tied to gold, meaning that it had a fixed value in relation to gold. One ounce of gold was worth $35.

- Other countries' currencies were ' pegged to the U.S. dollar.' It meant that instead of being directly linked to gold, currencies like the British pound or the French franc were tied to the value of the U.S. dollar. Central banks could exchange their currencies for U.S. dollars, and the U.S. promised that anyone holding dollars could exchange them for gold at a fixed rate.

This system made the U.S. dollar the foundation of international trade and finance. Countries trusted the dollar because the United States's gold reserves backed it, and its stability helped facilitate international transactions.

Over time, many nations began to hold large reserves of U.S. dollars as a safety net, knowing that the dollar's value was reliable.

The Dollar's Reign After Bretton Woods

The Bretton Woods system worked well for a time, but by the late 1960s and early 1970s, it began to show signs of strain. As the U.S. spent heavily on domestic programs and the Vietnam War, the supply of dollars in circulation far exceeded the gold reserves held by the U.S. Other countries began questioning whether the U.S. could fulfill its promise to exchange dollars for gold.

In 1971, facing a potential run on U.S. gold reserves, President Richard Nixon made the dramatic decision to end the dollar's convertibility into gold. This effectively ended the Bretton Woods system and ushered in a new era of fiat money—currency not backed by a physical commodity like gold but by the TRUST and authority of the issuing government.

Despite the collapse of the gold standard, the U.S. dollar remained the world's most important currency. Why? The U.S. economy was still the largest globally, and the dollar was deeply ingrained in the global financial system.

Additionally, many international contracts and trade deals were denominated in U.S. dollars, reinforcing the dollar's central role.

Why the Dollar Still Remains Dominant

Even today, decades after the end of the gold standard, the U.S. dollar continues to dominate global finance. This status is known as being the 'world's reserve currency,' and it carries several benefits for the United States:

- Lower borrowing costs: Because many countries and investors want to hold U.S. dollars, the U.S. government can borrow money at lower interest rates. The U.S. can borrow its own currency, reducing the risk of foreign exchange fluctuations.

- International trade dominance: The dollar is used in significant international trade. For example, oil, often called 'black gold,' is primarily traded in U.S. dollars. This reinforces the dollar's importance, as countries need dollars to purchase oil and other vital commodities.

- Global stability: Central banks worldwide hold large U.S. dollar reserves as part of their foreign exchange reserves, helping countries stabilize their currencies during economic uncertainty.

According to the International Monetary Fund (IMF), in 2020, the U.S. dollar accounted for approximately 60% of global foreign exchange reserves. This means that central banks worldwide continue to hold most of their foreign currency reserves in U.S. dollars, reinforcing the dollar's dominance in global finance.

Challenges to the Dollar's Status

However, the dollar's position as the world's reserve currency is not without challenges. In recent years, some countries have expressed interest in reducing their reliance on the U.S. dollar. For example, nations like India, China, and Russia have sought to conduct more of their trade in currencies other than the dollar to reduce their exposure to U.S. economic policies.

The rise of digital currencies, like Bitcoin and central bank digital currencies (CBDCs), also presents potential alternatives to traditional currencies. While these digital currencies are still in their infancy, they represent a future where new forms of money could challenge the dominance of the U.S. dollar.

The Dollar's Future: Still the King of Cash or Ready to Pass the Crown?

The U.S. dollar has had a wild ride since the Bretton Woods Agreement, and it's still rocking as the world's go-to currency. While there are some challenges to its dominance, the dollar has much going for it. It's widely used around the globe, and with the U.S. economy being one of the strongest, the dollar stays front and centre in the global money game.

Sure, some people think other currencies like the Euro or the Chinese Yuan might step in, but for now, the dollar is like the MVP of the world economy – dependable, strong, and tough to beat. It's the currency everyone trusts, whether you're trading oil or buying gadgets.

As long as the U.S. stays a key player in the world economy, the dollar's reign isn't going anywhere anytime soon. Other currencies might challenge it, but the dollar is still the leading player on which everyone is betting.

Understanding the history of the U.S. dollar's rise to prominence helps us see how interconnected the world's economies have become—and how crucial the dollar remains in shaping our financial future.

6

The Gold Standard—A Golden Era for Money?

For much of modern history, money was not simply pieces of paper or digital numbers on a screen—it was backed by something tangible and universally valued: gold. This system, known as the 'gold standard,' linked the value of a country's currency directly to its gold reserves, ensuring that money had an intrinsic value. In other words, if you held a dollar bill, you could technically exchange it for a specific amount of gold.

The gold standard provided stability and trust in the monetary system but also had limitations that eventually led to its downfall. Understanding the gold standard is essential to grasp how money has evolved and why modern currencies, like the U.S. dollar, function the way they do today.

What Was the Gold Standard?

The gold standard was a system in which the value of a nation's currency was directly tied to a certain amount of gold. Under this system, countries had to hold gold reserves, and individuals could exchange their paper money for a fixed quantity of gold. This gave people confidence in the value of their money since it was backed by a physical asset that humans had prized for thousands of years.

For example, in 1834, one U.S. dollar was equivalent to 1/20 of an ounce of gold. This meant that if you had $20, you could walk into a bank and trade it for an ounce of gold.

The gold standard became popular in the 19th century, and by the early 20th century, it was the dominant monetary system used by most of the world's major economies. It offered several vital benefits:

- Stability: The gold standard provided a stable monetary base, as the money supply was limited by the amount of gold a country possessed. This kept inflation in check and gave people confidence that the value of their money would not suddenly plummet.

- Trust in currency: Because gold was a universally recognized store of value, domestically and internationally, currencies backed by gold were considered trustworthy and reliable.

The Challenges of the Gold Standard

While the gold standard had its advantages, it also posed significant challenges—especially during war or economic crises. One of the main issues was that the system placed strict limits on how much money a country could print.

Since the amount of money in circulation had to be tied to the amount of gold held in reserve, governments needed more flexibility in managing their economies. Consider a few examples :

- World War I: When World War I broke out, countries faced enormous financial pressures. Governments needed to spend vast amounts of money on their militaries and other war-related expenses. However, under the gold standard, they were limited in how much currency they could issue. Many countries, including the United Kingdom and Germany, suspended the gold standard during the war to print more money to fund their war efforts. After the war, these countries struggled to return to the gold standard, as their economies were weakened and their gold reserves depleted.

- The Great Depression: The gold standard also contributed to the deepening of the Great Depression of the 1930s. As economies worldwide collapsed and unemployment soared, governments could not respond effectively because they were tied to the gold standard. Countries couldn't print more money or devalue their currencies to stimulate economic growth, leading to a prolonged and severe global financial crisis.

Moving Away from Gold

By the early 20th century, the limitations of the gold standard were becoming increasingly apparent. While the system had provided stability in the 19th century, the pressures of modern economies, global wars, and financial crises made it difficult for countries to maintain.

The connection between the dollar and gold weakened in the early 20th century in the United States. In 1933, during the depths of the Great Depression, President Franklin D. Roosevelt took significant steps to loosen the U.S. economy's reliance on gold. He banned private ownership of gold and stopped the direct convertibility of dollars into gold, effectively taking the U.S. off the gold standard for domestic purposes.

However, the dollar was still tied to gold in international transactions, and foreign governments could exchange their dollars for gold.

The final blow to the gold standard came in 1971 when President Richard Nixon made the historic decision to end the U.S. dollar's convertibility into gold altogether. This move, known as the 'Nixon Shock,' effectively marked the end of the global gold standard.

Under increasing pressure from inflation and trade imbalances, the U.S. government decided it could no longer afford to maintain the dollar's link to gold.

Why Did the Gold Standard End?

The decision to abandon the gold standard was not taken lightly. It resulted from mounting economic pressures that had been building for years. By the 1960s, the U.S. economy faced significant challenges, including the costs of the Vietnam War and the expanding welfare state under President Lyndon B. Johnson.

These expenditures strained U.S. gold reserves, as more dollars were being printed without a corresponding increase in gold holdings.

Foreign countries, particularly those with large dollar reserves like France, grew concerned about the U.S.'s ability to maintain the gold standard. Some nations started demanding gold in exchange for their dollars, further depleting U.S. gold reserves.

In 1971, facing a potential run on U.S. gold reserves, Nixon announced that the U.S. would no longer honor the agreement to exchange dollars for gold.

This decision ended the era of the gold standard. It ushered in a new system of fiat money, where the value of a currency is based not on a physical commodity like gold but on TRUST in the government that issues it.

The Legacy of the Gold Standard

The end of the gold standard marked the beginning of the modern financial system, in which currencies are not tied to any physical asset. While this new system offers governments more flexibility to manage their economies, it also means that the value of money is now based on trust in governments and central banks rather than a tangible resource like gold.

Many economists believe moving away from the gold standard was necessary for economic growth and stability in the modern world. However, some critics argue that fiat money systems are more prone to inflation and financial instability because they are not anchored to a physical asset like gold.

Despite its end, the gold standard still holds a certain mystique in popular culture and economic theory. Some even advocate for a return to the gold standard to restore discipline to the global financial system. However, most economists agree that such a move would be impractical in today's complex, interconnected world.

From Gold to TRUST

With its promise of stability and inherent value, the gold standard shaped the global economy for centuries. However, as the demands of modern economies grew, the limitations of gold became clear. Today, we live in a fiat money world, where currency's value is based on trust rather than tangible resources.

Understanding the rise and fall of the gold standard provides valuable insight into how money works and why governments make the decisions they do about monetary policy.

7

The End of the Gold Standard and the Rise of Fiat Money

Under the existing gold standard, foreign governments could exchange their U.S. dollars for gold at a fixed rate of $35 per ounce. However, the growing number of dollars in circulation led to fears that the U.S. didn't have enough gold reserves to cover its obligations.

Countries like France, under President Charles de Gaulle, began demanding gold in exchange for their dollars, depleting U.S. gold reserves.

To prevent a run on U.S. gold, the US government decided to sever the link between the dollar and gold, effectively transitioning the U.S. and the world from the gold standard to a 'fiat currency system.' In the announcement, it was framed as a temporary measure to defend the dollar against "international speculators," but it marked the permanent end of gold-backed money.

What is Fiat Currency?

In a fiat currency system, money is not backed by any tangible asset. Instead, the value of a currency is determined by the government that issues it and by the public's TRUST in that government. Essentially, money has value because people believe it has value.

Here's what distinguishes fiat currency from the gold standard:
- No physical backing: Fiat money, such as the U.S. dollar today, has no intrinsic value. It cannot be exchanged for a set amount of gold or any other physical commodity.
- Government control: The supply of fiat currency is controlled by the government or central banks like the Federal Reserve in the U.S. This allows governments to print more money or adjust interest rates to manage the economy.
- Trust-based value: The value of fiat currency depends on public trust. If people lose faith in the government or central bank that issues the currency, its value can decrease rapidly.

The Immediate Impact of the End of the Gold Standard

At first, the decision to end the dollar's link to gold seemed to solve some pressing problems. Without maintaining gold reserves for every dollar in circulation, the U.S. government gained more flexibility in managing the economy. It could print more money to fund government programs or stimulate economic growth without worrying about depleting its gold reserves.

The decision also allowed the Federal Reserve to play a more active role in regulating the economy. By adjusting interest rates and controlling the money supply, the Fed could more effectively influence inflation, unemployment, and economic growth.

However, this newfound freedom also came with risks. Since

the value of fiat money is not based on a physical asset like gold, it is more vulnerable to inflation. If a government prints too much money, it can reduce the currency's purchasing power, leading to rising prices and economic instability.

The Risks and Rewards of Fiat Currency

The decision to end the gold standard opened the door to a new era of monetary policy and created challenges that continue to shape today's global economy.

The Benefits:

- Flexibility in Economic Policy: One of the primary advantages of a fiat currency system is that it gives governments and central banks more tools to manage the economy.

For example, central banks can lower interest rates during recessions or increase the money supply to encourage borrowing and spending, which can help boost economic growth.

-No Constraints on Money Supply: Under the gold standard, a country's gold reserves limited the amount of money in circulation. With fiat money, governments can issue more currency as needed, which can help address immediate economic needs, such as funding infrastructure projects or responding to crises like wars or natural disasters.

The Risks:

- Inflation: Without the discipline of the gold standard, governments can sometimes be tempted to print too much money, leading to inflation.

A well-known example is 'hyperinflation' in Zimbabwe in the early 2000s, where excessive money printing led to astronomical price increases and rendered the Zimbabwean dollar nearly worthless.

- Trust and Stability: Fiat money's value is primarily based on trust in the government and its ability to manage the economy. The currency's value can plummet if that trust erodes due to political instability, poor economic management, or other factors.

For instance, during the 2008 financial crisis, the U.S. government had to take extraordinary measures to restore confidence in the dollar and the global economic system.

The Long-Term Effects of Delinking the Dollar from Gold

The decision to end the gold standard had profound and lasting effects on the global financial system. The U.S. dollar, no longer constrained by gold, became the world's 'dominant reserve currency,' used in international trade and held by central banks worldwide as part of their foreign exchange reserves.

However, it also shifted the global economy into an era where inflation, currency devaluation, and financial crises became more frequent concerns. Central banks now play a more critical role in managing economies. They control the money supply and set interest rates to balance inflation and growth.

In hindsight, the decision to end the gold standard was a turning point in modern economic history. While it allowed the U.S. government more flexibility to manage its economy, it also ushered in a new era of monetary policy that requires careful balancing to maintain trust and stability in the financial system.

8

The Rise of Digital Money and the Role of Banks

As we move further into the digital age, how we use and understand money has evolved dramatically. Gone are the days when most transactions required physical cash. Today, money often exists as digital entries in bank accounts, facilitating seamless online transactions, mobile payments, and instant transfers across the globe.

This shift to 'digital money' has changed how we interact with currency and transformed the role of banks in the financial system. We'll now explore how digital money works, commercial banks' role in creating it, and the system that makes it all possible—the 'fractional reserve system.'

The Shift to Digital Money

Digital money is simply money that exists electronically rather than physically, like coins or paper bills. While we may still carry some cash in our wallets, a growing number of transactions occur digitally. Think about the last time you purchased something online, paid for groceries with a credit card, or transferred money using a mobile app—these are all examples of digital money in action.

Digital money offers several advantages:
   - Convenience: No need to carry large amounts of cash or worry about exact change.
   - Speed: Payments can be made instantly, whether you're transferring money to a friend or paying for a product.
   - Security: Digital transactions often have layers of encryption and security, making it safer than carrying physical cash that could be lost or stolen.

This shift towards digital money has also given rise to innovations like 'cryptocurrencies,' such as Bitcoin, which further remove the need for physical currency. Although cryptocurrencies are still in their early stages of adoption, they are part of the growing landscape of digital money that is redefining the global economy.

The Role of Commercial Banks

As more of our money exists digitally, commercial banks have become central players in the financial system. Banks are responsible for holding our deposits and 'creating new money'—primarily through lending. This process is a cornerstone of modern banking and is made possible by a system known as 'fractional reserve banking.'

In a nutshell, when you deposit money into a bank, it doesn't keep all of it in a vault. Instead, under the fractional reserve system, banks are only required to hold a small fraction of their customers' deposits in reserve. The rest is lent out to borrowers. This system allows banks to multiply the amount of money in circulation by effectively 'creating new money' with every loan they issue.

How Fractional Reserve Banking Works

Imagine you deposit $1,000 into your bank account. The bank must keep a specific percentage of that deposit (say 10%) on hand, called the reserve requirement. In this case, the bank would hold $100 in reserve and could lend out the remaining $900 to someone else. That borrower might then use the $900 to buy something, and the seller might deposit that $900 into their bank.

The process repeats, with each bank keeping a portion of the deposit in reserve and lending out the rest. In this way, the initial $1,000 deposit can generate multiple loans, effectively creating more money in the economy.

Here's something cool

When a bank gives out a loan, it doesn't hand you a suitcase full of cash. Instead, the money is created digitally, like magic numbers that pop up in your bank account. It's all done on a computer screen—no physical money changes hands. As you repay the loan, that digital money disappears like it was never really there!

But here's the kicker: you're also paying interest on the loan. That interest is how the bank makes its profit. So, the bank may erase the loan amount, but the extra cash (the interest) goes straight into their pockets!

The Benefits and Risks of Fractional Reserve Banking

Fractional reserve banking plays a critical role in the modern economy. It enables banks to lend more money than they physically hold.

Key Benefits:

- Increased economic activity: By lending money, banks help businesses grow, fund new projects, and enable consumers to make large purchases like homes or cars. This lending stimulates economic growth.

- Access to credit: Consumers and businesses can borrow the money they need for investments, such as starting a new business or buying a house.

Certain Risks:

- Bank runs: If too many people try to withdraw their money at once—perhaps due to a loss of confidence in the bank—the bank might not have enough reserves to cover all the withdrawals. This can lead to a 'bank run,' where the bank collapses because it cannot meet the demands of its customers.

- Risk of over-lending: If banks lend too freely, they may give loans to people or businesses that can't repay them, leading to financial instability. This was seen during the 2008 financial crisis, when banks made risky loans, leading to widespread defaults and the collapse of the housing market.

Governments and central banks closely monitor the banking system and implement regulations to mitigate these risks. For example, the Federal Reserve in the U.S. sets the reserve requirement and adjusts it based on economic conditions. Additionally, banks must hold a portion of their assets in highly liquid forms, such as government bonds, to ensure they can meet withdrawal demands.

The Future of Digital Money

As technology advances, we'll likely see even more innovations in how money is used and managed. Digital wallets, UPI, mobile banking apps, and even cryptocurrencies are becoming more common, offering consumers more ways to manage their finances.

Central Bank Digital Currencies (CBDCs) are also gaining attention. These digital versions of national currencies are issued and regulated by central banks. Countries like China are already testing digital versions of their currency, and other nations are exploring similar projects. CBDCs offer a more secure and efficient alternative to cash and provide central banks with new tools to manage the economy.

The shift to digital money also raises important questions about privacy and security. As our financial lives move online, ensuring digital transactions remain secure from cyber threats will be a top priority for governments and financial institutions.

A New Era for Money and Banks

The rise of digital money has transformed how we interact with our finances, making transactions faster, easier, and more convenient. Fractional reserve banking plays a vital role in this system by creating new money and providing access to credit. However, this system also introduces certain risks, requiring careful oversight and regulation.

As we move into the future, digital money will likely continue to evolve, with new technologies like cryptocurrencies and central bank digital currencies offering exciting possibilities. But no matter how money changes, the core principles of trust, security, and responsible lending will remain crucial to the financial system's stability.

9

The Crypto Revolution: Challenging Traditional Money

Over the last decade, a new form of money has captured the world's attention—cryptocurrency. Starting with Bitcoin in 2009, this digital currency has sparked debates, raised hopes, and challenged the traditional monetary systems we've relied on for centuries. But how did cryptocurrencies rise to prominence, and what makes them different from the money we use daily? Let's explore.

The Emergence of Bitcoin and Other Cryptocurrencies

In the wake of the 2008 financial crisis, trust in banks and government-backed currencies was at an all-time low. Many questioned the traditional financial system's ability to protect people's money, leading to the birth of Bitcoin. Created by an anonymous figure known as Satoshi Nakamoto, Bitcoin was introduced as the world's first decentralized digital currency. Unlike dollars, euros, or yen, Bitcoin wasn't controlled by any government or central bank. Instead, it relied on a peer-to-peer network, allowing people to transfer money directly to one another without needing an intermediary like a bank.

Bitcoin paved the way for thousands of other cryptocurrencies to emerge. Today, digital currencies such as Ethereum, Litecoin, and Ripple are household names, each with unique features. For example, while Bitcoin is often compared to digital gold due to its limited supply and store of value function, Ethereum is known for enabling "smart contracts," self-executing contracts with the terms of the agreement directly written into code. These digital assets operate on 'Blockchain Technology,' which is the backbone of the crypto revolution.

How Crypto Challenges Traditional Money

Cryptocurrencies challenge the very definition of money as we know it. Traditionally, money is issued by governments and backed by central banks, meaning its value is tied to a country's economic policies. Cryptocurrencies, however, are not tied to any single economy or institution. Their value is determined by supply and demand and often by the belief in the underlying technology.

One of the most significant advantages of cryptocurrencies is their potential for financial inclusion. Around the world, billions of people lack access to traditional banking systems due to geography or lack of resources. Cryptocurrencies offer an alternative—anyone with an internet connection can send and receive digital money without a bank account.

But with this innovation come challenges. Cryptocurrencies are highly volatile—one day, the value of Bitcoin could skyrocket, and the next, it could plummet. Unlike fiat money, which is typically stabilized by government policies, cryptocurrencies are more susceptible to speculation and market forces. This makes them both exciting for investors and risky for everyday users!

Additionally, the decentralized nature of cryptocurrencies means there's no central authority to intervene if something goes wrong. If you forget your crypto wallet's password or it's hacked, there's no customer service line to call for help. This lack of regulation is both a draw and a drawback for users, depending on how much control they want over their assets.

Blockchain Technology and Its Potential

At the heart of every cryptocurrency is blockchain technology. A blockchain is a digital ledger that records transactions with a particular cryptocurrency. This ledger is unique because it's decentralized—no single person or organization controls it. Instead, it's maintained by a network of computers worldwide, making it incredibly secure and resistant to tampering.

Each transaction made on the blockchain is grouped into a "block" and added to the chain in chronological order. Once a block is added, it cannot be changed, which makes blockchain highly transparent and trustworthy. This transparency is one of the reasons why many people believe blockchain technology could be used for more than just cryptocurrencies. Its applications could range from secure voting systems to transparent supply chains in industries like food and medicine.

Major companies and governments are already exploring ways to incorporate blockchain into their operations. For example, IBM and Walmart use blockchain to track the origin of food products, ensuring quality and safety. By providing an unchangeable record of a product's journey, blockchain can help consumers trust that the food they eat is safe and ethically sourced.

The Future of Cryptocurrencies?

Cryptocurrencies and blockchain technology represent a bold new frontier in the world of finance. They have the potential to disrupt traditional systems, offer new opportunities for financial inclusion, and create more secure and transparent ways of doing business. However, challenges remain, from volatility to regulation. As governments, businesses, and individuals adapt to this rapidly changing landscape, one thing is clear—cryptocurrency is here to stay, and it's already transforming how we think about money.

10

Chapter 10

The world of money is undergoing a radical transformation. From the convenience of digital payments to the rise of cryptocurrencies, how we think about and use money is evolving faster than ever. Physical cash, once the cornerstone of global commerce, now seems to be slowly fading into the background. As technology advances, governments are exploring new forms of money, like Central Bank Digital Currencies (CBDCs), while cryptocurrencies continue to gain traction. The future of money is at a crossroads, and young people today will play a critical role in shaping it.

The Rise of Digital Payments

In recent years, digital payments have become an everyday part of life. Whether using a mobile app to pay for a coffee or sending money to a friend through a peer-to-peer platform, the convenience of digital transactions is undeniable. Countries like India, Sweden, and China are already moving toward becoming cashless societies, where the vast majority of payments are made electronically.

One reason for this shift is the increasing reliance on smartphones and digital platforms. People can complete transactions with just a few taps, often with greater security than carrying physical cash. For businesses, digital payments reduce the need to handle large amounts of currency, which lowers the risks associated with theft or counterfeiting.

Digital payments have also revolutionized access to banking services for people lacking them. In countries where traditional banks are few and far between, mobile payment systems are helping millions of people participate in the economy for the first time. Platforms like M-Pesa in Kenya, GPay, and Paytm in India allow users to save, send, and receive money using only a basic mobile phone, revolutionizing access to financial services.

Alternate Currencies and the Future of Finance

While CBDCs represent government-backed digital currencies, cryptocurrencies like Bitcoin and Ethereum offer an entirely different vision of the future of money. These decentralized currencies are not controlled by any central authority, making them attractive to people who distrust traditional financial systems or seek more control over their assets.

Cryptocurrencies have already had a significant impact on the world of finance. Companies like Tesla and PayPal have begun accepting Bitcoin for payments, and even major financial institutions are starting to invest in cryptocurrency. For some, cryptocurrencies represent the next step in the evolution of money—one that could potentially eliminate the need for banks and allow people to manage their wealth directly.

However, cryptocurrencies are still in their early stages and face significant challenges. Their value can be highly volatile, with prices skyrocketing one day and crashing the next. There are also concerns about security and the potential for fraud, especially in unregulated markets. Governments worldwide are grappling with how to regulate cryptocurrencies while encouraging innovation.

Despite these challenges, many experts believe cryptocurrencies will play a vital role in the future of finance. Blockchain technology, which underpins most cryptocurrencies, offers secure, transparent transactions that could be applied to industries beyond finance, such as supply chain management and voting systems.

What Does the Future Hold?

As the world moves further into the digital age, it's clear that money will continue to evolve. The idea of 'physical cash becoming obsolete' is no longer just a distant possibility—it's a real question that governments, businesses, and individuals are beginning to face.

Understanding these changes will be crucial for young people. As new technologies emerge and reshape how money is used and managed, those equipped with knowledge of digital currencies, blockchain, and the evolving financial landscape will have a significant advantage in navigating the world of tomorrow.

The future of money is still being written, and while we may not yet know precisely what it will look like, one thing is sure: the rules of money are changing. Staying informed and adaptable will be vital for young minds to thrive in this new financial world.

11

The Shift Away from the U.S. Dollar – A Changing Global Landscape

As we read earlier, the U.S. dollar has been the undisputed leader in the global financial system for decades. Serving as the world's 'reserve currency,' the dollar has been a symbol of stability, widely used in international trade, and held in significant quantities by central banks across the globe.

However, recent trends indicate that the dollar's dominance is less secure than it once was. Countries like China, India, and others are starting to explore alternatives, raising questions about the future of the global monetary system. Could we witness the early stages of a world where the U.S. dollar no longer reigns supreme?

The Dollar's Role in Global Finance

Even after the gold standard was abandoned in the 1970s, the dollar remained the world's dominant currency. Today, the dollar is used in about 60% of global foreign exchange reserves and is involved in roughly 88% of all international transactions.

The dollar's status as the world's reserve currency gives the U.S. significant economic advantages. It allows the country to borrow at lower costs and offers U.S. companies and consumers access to cheaper goods and services from abroad. In many ways, the dollar's dominance has reinforced the U.S.'s political and economic power on the global stage.

Emerging Economies and the Rise of Alternatives

However, in recent years, emerging economies like China and India have begun exploring alternatives to the dollar. These nations want to diversify their reserves, reducing their reliance on the U.S. currency by investing in other assets and using regional currencies for trade. This shift is motivated by economic and geopolitical considerations, as some countries seek to reduce the U.S. influence over their financial systems.

One of the most significant developments in this regard is the rise of China's Renminbi (RMB). Over the last decade, China has worked to internationalize its currency, making it more widely used in global trade and financial transactions. China's massive infrastructure and investment program, the 'Belt and Road Initiative,' has also promoted the RMB. Countries participating in this initiative increasingly use the renminbi for trade and loans, helping China position its currency as a viable alternative to the dollar.

In 2016, the International Monetary Fund (IMF) added the renminbi to its 'Special Drawing Rights' (SDR) basket, a milestone officially recognizing the RMB as one of the world's major currencies, alongside the dollar, euro, yen, and British pound. This was a clear signal that China's currency was becoming more integrated into the global financial system.

Regional Currency Agreements and Diversification

Another critical factor in the potential shift away from the dollar is the rise of regional currency agreements. Countries within regions like Asia and Europe are increasingly conducting trade using their own currencies instead of defaulting to the U.S. dollar. For example, India and Russia have made agreements to trade in their respective currencies, bypassing the dollar entirely. Similarly, nations within the Association of Southeast Asian Nations (ASEAN) have been exploring mechanisms to facilitate trade using regional currencies.

These moves reflect a desire to reduce dependence on the dollar, particularly in light of economic sanctions and political tensions that sometimes arise between the U.S. and other nations. By diversifying their currency reserves and trade mechanisms, countries protect themselves from potential vulnerabilities and signal their growing independence from the U.S.-dominated global order.

Geopolitical and Economic Implications

The potential decline of the U.S. dollar as the dominant global currency would have significant implications for the global economy and geopolitics. If more countries move away from the dollar, the U.S. could lose some of the economic privileges of issuing the world's reserve currency. For instance, the U.S. might find borrowing money or financing trade deficits more expensive.

At the same time, a world with multiple reserve currencies could be more complex and less stable. The dollar's dominance provides predictability and liquidity in global markets, which could be more challenging to maintain with several competing currencies. Additionally, the shift away from the dollar could alter the balance of power between nations as countries like China and others gain more influence in global financial institutions.

What Does the Future Hold for the U.S. Dollar?

While it's too early to predict the end of the U.S. dollar's dominance, the global financial system is evolving. The rise of China's renminbi, the growth of regional currency agreements, and the diversification of foreign reserves are all signs that the world is moving toward a more multipolar currency system.

Understanding these shifts is crucial for young people. The world of finance is no longer dominated by just one currency, and as emerging economies grow in influence, the global monetary system will likely continue to evolve. In the future, a firm grasp of multiple currencies, including digital and decentralized forms of money, could be essential for navigating this increasingly complex landscape.

The shift away from the dollar may not happen overnight, but the signs remain. As countries continue to explore alternatives, the global financial system may soon look very different from the one we know today.

12

Mastering Money in a Choppy World – Your Guide to Financial Success

Managing money effectively is more important than ever in today's fast-paced, ever-evolving world. As we grow up, our financial choices can shape our future—affecting everything from our daily expenses to long-term goals like buying a home, starting a business, or traveling the world. This is why financial literacy, or the ability to understand and make informed decisions about money, is such a critical skill.

Whether you realize it or not, money plays a role in almost every aspect of your life. Learning how to manage it now can set you on the path to success and help you avoid mistakes many people make when they don't fully understand how money works.

But where do you start? As a teenager, you might not have a job yet, but chances are you've received money in some form—perhaps as a gift, an allowance, or from doing small jobs. You've probably also had to decide how to spend that money, whether it was on snacks, a new game, or saving up for something more extensive like a bike or a phone.

This is where basic financial skills come in. Budgeting, for example, is one of the most important skills. It means planning how to spend your money wisely and making sure you don't run out before you've covered everything you need.

Let's look at an example. Imagine you have $50 and need to decide how to use it for the next two weeks. You could spend it all in one day on something fun, like going to the movies and grabbing some snacks, but then you'd have nothing left for the rest of the week.

On the other hand, if you create a budget, you could allocate $10 for entertainment and $10 for snacks and save $30 for something bigger you're working toward. By budgeting, you're making sure you don't waste all your money at once and teaching yourself discipline—a skill that will be crucial when you start managing more significant amounts of money in the future.

Now, let's explore an activity to help you practice. Set a savings goal, such as buying a new video game or gadget, and figure out how much it costs. Then, create a budget plan based on any income you have, like allowance or birthday money. For example, if the item costs $100, and you receive $20 a month, calculate how long it will take you to save up if you set aside a certain portion of your income.

This process will teach you the importance of patience and the value of making smart financial decisions. By building your financial knowledge now, you'll be better prepared for the more significant decisions you'll face in the future.

The Importance of Financial Literacy

Financial literacy isn't just for adults; it's essential for anyone who wants to make intelligent decisions about their money. The earlier you start, the better. Having a firm grasp of personal finance will help you manage your income, save for important goals, and avoid costly mistakes like accumulating unnecessary debt.

For example, have you ever wondered why some people seem to have no trouble handling their money while others struggle with endless bills and credit card debt? It's often because they learned how to manage their money effectively early. Financially literate people understand budgeting, compound interest, and investing, allowing them to make informed choices that benefit their future.

Creating a Budget – Your First Step Toward Control

Budgeting is the foundation of money management. A budget helps you track what comes in (your income) and what goes out (your expenses). Many people, especially teenagers, might think budgeting is only necessary when you start earning a full-time salary, but it's valuable at any age. Budgeting can help you understand your spending habits and make better decisions, whether managing an allowance or a part-time job.

Here's a simple way to start budgeting:

- Track Your Spending: Record every dollar you spend over a month, whether on food, clothing, or entertainment. Apps like Mint or You Need a Budget (YNAB) make this easy.
- Set Categories: Break down your expenses into categories like food, transportation, entertainment, and savings. This will show you where your money is going and where you might be

able to cut back.

- Set Limits: Once you know how much you spend in each category, create limits for each one based on your income. For example, you might limit yourself to $50 a month for entertainment, leaving more money for savings or future goals.

Budgeting gives you control over your money instead of letting it control you. It lets you prioritize your spending and ensure you live within your means.

The Power of Saving – Why Starting Early Matters

One of the most important lessons in money management is the power of saving. Whether you're saving for something immediate like a new phone or something long-term like college, setting aside money regularly is crucial to reaching your goals. But saving is more than just putting money away—it's about developing a habit that will benefit you for years.

A simple savings strategy is the 50/30/20 rule:
- 50% of your income goes to needs (essential expenses like food, rent, and transportation).
- 30% goes to wants (entertainment, dining out, and hobbies).
- 20% goes to savings and investments.

By committing to save even a tiny portion of your income, you can build a financial safety net that will protect you in emergencies and help you achieve bigger goals over time.

Investing – Growing Your Money Over Time

Investing is one of the most effective ways to grow your wealth over time, but it's a concept that many young people find intimidating. However, you don't need to be an expert to start investing. The earlier you begin, the more you can take advantage of the power of compounding, where your earnings generate even more over time.

For example, if you invest $1,000 when you're 18 and earn an average return of 7% per year, that money could grow to over $7,600 by the time you're 50, even if you never add another penny. That's the power of time and compound interest!

There are many ways to invest, from simple savings accounts to fixed deposits, mutual funds, stocks, and bonds. Researching and finding investments that fit your goals and risk tolerance is essential. Online tools like Acorns or Robinhood make investing accessible for beginners, helping you build wealth with small, manageable contributions.

Avoiding Debt – A Key to Financial Freedom

One of the biggest challenges young people face is avoiding the trap of debt. Credit cards, student loans, and car payments can quickly add up, overwhelming you. While some debt, like student loans, can be a valuable investment in your future, other types, like credit card debt, can lead to high-interest payments and financial stress.

Here's how to manage debt wisely:

- Use Credit Sparingly: Credit cards can help build credit, but only if you pay off the balance each month. Carrying a balance can lead to high-interest charges that quickly spiral out of control.

- Understand Your Loans: If you take out student loans, ensure you understand the terms, including the interest rate and repayment schedule. Consider paying off interest while you're still in school to reduce the total amount you owe later.

Tools and Resources – Taking Charge of Your Financial Future

In today's digital world, countless resources are available to help you manage your money. From budgeting apps to investment platforms, you have access to tools that make managing your finances more effortless than ever. Take advantage of free online courses, financial blogs, and podcasts to continue learning about money management.

Financial literacy is not something you learn overnight—it's an ongoing process. But by starting now, you're building the skills that will set you up for success in an increasingly complex world.

Your Financial Journey Starts Now

Managing money in a changing world can feel daunting. Still, you can set yourself up for long-term financial success by focusing on budgeting, saving, investing, and avoiding debt. The world of money constantly evolves, but the skills the young minds build today will serve them for a lifetime. Take control of your financial future and watch as the possibilities open up.

13

Money, Price, Inflation, Banks, and You – How Money and Economics Shape Your World

One of the most critical ways money impacts everyday life is through inflation and interest rates. Have you ever noticed how prices rise over time? That's inflation, which means the same amount of money buys less than it used to. Inflation affects everyone—from the cost of your favourite snack to how much a business spends on supplies.

Interest rates, which banks charge for lending money, are another major player. If you borrow money to buy something today, you'll need to pay it back with interest—so the cost of borrowing money affects spending and saving habits. Try to dig into Federal Open Market Committee (FOMC) meetings of the Fed- how the tweaking of interest rates by the Fed affects the economy and Wall Street and the world at large.

Banks are vital to making this system work. They keep your

money safe and lend it out to people and businesses to help them grow. This lending fuels the economy by allowing people to start businesses, buy homes, or attend school. But banks aren't the only players—central banks, like the Federal Reserve in the U.S., make decisions that can affect an entire country's economy by controlling interest rates and the amount of money in circulation. Visit the website of any bank, click every tab on the website for over a few weeks, and make some notes daily.

On a larger scale, money doesn't just stay within one country's borders. In a global economy, currencies are exchanged, and their values fluctuate based on a country's economic health. A strong economy boosts its currency, while a weaker economy can see its currency's value drop. This affects international trade and the prices of imported goods, like electronics or clothes made overseas.

Money isn't just about numbers—it's about how a country grows, how businesses succeed, and how individuals like you thrive. A stable economy leads to better job opportunities, higher incomes, and improved living standards. That's why understanding the relationship between money and economics matters. It shapes the choices you make today and your future as part of a global, interconnected world.

Price: The Invisible Hand That Rules the World

Ever wondered why a new phone costs so much or why snack prices go up at the school canteen? It's all about price, which is like the referee in the global economy. Prices are set by a combination of supply (how much stuff is available) and demand (how much people want it). If everyone's dying to get the latest sneakers, prices shoot up. The price drops like a rock if nobody cares about last season's shoes.

Prices do more than just help you decide what to buy—they keep the world economy fair and balanced. They're like the invisible hand that helps businesses and consumers make smart choices. No matter where you live, prices create a level playing field. If a product is too expensive, buyers look elsewhere, which forces companies to compete. That's why prices for most things are roughly the same everywhere, from jeans in Japan to burgers in Brazil.

In the end, price isn't just about what you pay—it's how the economy talks to itself, adjusting for what's needed and where it's needed and making sure everyone gets a fair shot, whether you're buying, selling, or saving.

To a young mind, money might seem tricky, but mastering basics like inflation, interest rates, and prices can level up your financial game.

- Inflation? It's why saving smart is key—your money won't stretch as far in the future.
- Interest rates? If you borrow for a car or college one day, you'll owe more than you borrowed, so plan ahead! And that shiny new product?
- Price? It is set by Supply and demand, so waiting might get you a deal. Learn these now, and you'll be making money moves that your future self will thank you for!

Here, I can see that you are getting motivated to learn the basics of Microeconomics and Macroeconomics.

Go ahead, Do that!

14

Conclusion– Young Minds Embracing a New Financial World

Do not read this chapter if you claim to have read the previous chapters sincerely but if you claim to have read the book so far thoroughly, you must read this chapter to varify your claim!

As we wrap up our journey through the complex yet fascinating world of money, it's clear that we stand on the edge of a financial revolution. The evolution of money has shown just how adaptable and inventive human societies can be when it comes to managing value and trade. Now, as new technologies and shifting global economies continue to reshape the landscape, the future of money is more uncertain—and more exciting—than ever before.

The Changing Face of Money

In the past few decades alone, the concept of money has undergone significant transformation. Once the most tangible form of money, digital payments increasingly replace physical cash. From mobile wallets to contactless cards, how we pay for goods and services is becoming faster, more convenient, and often invisible to the eye.

Consider the rise of digital payment systems like PayPal, Venmo, UPI, and Apple Pay. These technologies have enabled people to transfer money to one another almost instantaneously without needing physical currency. A teenager in one country can pay for a video game created by a developer halfway across the world in seconds—all through digital means.

But these changes extend far beyond convenience. With the emergence of blockchain technology, cryptocurrencies like Bitcoin and Ethereum are challenging traditional notions of money and finance. These digital currencies operate outside the control of governments and central banks, offering people new ways to exchange value across borders. Though still in their early stages, cryptocurrencies have sparked debates about the future role of government-backed money and the potential for a decentralised global financial system.

Understanding the Past to Prepare for the Future

To fully appreciate where money is headed, it's essential to understand its past. This book has taken young minds on a journey through the history of money, from the early barter systems to the creation of the U.S. dollar as the world's dominant currency. Along the way, we've explored the rise and fall of the gold standard, the importance of financial literacy, and the increasing role of digital money in everyday transactions.

The need for greater efficiency and flexibility drove each step in the evolution of money. Bartering was too complicated because it required a 'double coincidence of wants', and 'commodity money' (like salt or shells) lacked universal value.

Creating coins and paper money solved many of these problems by providing a consistent store of value. However, these forms of money were also limited, so we moved toward fiat currency—money backed by TRUST in governments rather than tangible commodities.

We are seeing a similar shift with the rise of digital currencies and assets. Cryptocurrencies, for instance, offer the possibility of a financial system that is faster, more transparent, and less reliant on centralized institutions.

At the same time, governments are experimenting with central bank digital currencies (CBDCs). These digital versions of national currencies could combine the benefits of digital money with the stability of state-backed assets. China has already begun testing its digital yuan, and other countries are following suit. In India, the CBDC(called the digital rupee) has been launched as a pilot initiative.

The Importance of Staying Informed

As these changes unfold, the rules of money will continue to evolve. For young people entering adulthood, staying informed about these developments is more important than ever. The financial world you will inherit is vastly different from that of your parents and grandparents. Understanding the difference between traditional currency and cryptocurrency, or knowing how digital payments and investments work, will be essential to making intelligent financial decisions.

For example, as the use of physical cash declines, new security measures will be needed to protect digital transactions. Cybersecurity and privacy concerns will become even more critical as money moves deeper into the digital realm.

Meanwhile, global political and economic events will still

CONCLUSION– YOUNG MINDS EMBRACING A NEW FINANCIAL WORLD

influence inflation, interest rates, and currency values—just as they always have. However, the tools we use to navigate these shifts will look very different from those of the past.

Your Role in the Financial Future

The knowledge you've gained throughout this book equips you to thrive in this changing world. Whether saving for a new Macbook Pro, planning for college, or thinking about your first investment, understanding how money works will give you an edge. As technology reshapes finance, you'll have the skills to adapt, make informed decisions, and stay ahead of the curve.

More than ever, financial literacy isn't just about balancing a checkbook or saving for retirement. It's about understanding how global economies interact, how digital currencies challenge traditional systems, and how to leverage these changes to your advantage.

Navigating a New World of Money

As we move forward, staying informed is crucial, as is adapting to new trends and embracing the opportunities presented by this rapidly changing landscape.

Your financial journey is just beginning, and the future of money promises to be as exciting as it is unpredictable. By taking control of your financial knowledge now, you're preparing yourself for a lifetime of intelligent decisions and economic success in a world where the only constant is change.

MONEY MATTERS: FOR YOUNG MINDS motivates you to learn more about money matters.

So, keep updating yourselves on Money Matters!

About the Author

The author is a seasoned engineer with over four decades of hands-on experience in the construction and infrastructure sector. In the second inning of my life, I have decided to enter the writing field. I have always been a voracious reader and am passionate about exploring diverse subjects, from fiction and history to personal development, investing, and philosophy.

Drawing on the disciplined approach of my engineering background, I craft narratives with precision, depth, and thoughtful attention to detail. I am particularly interested in exploring topics that challenge conventional thinking, provoke introspection, or offer new perspectives.

As I embark on this new chapter of my life, I am excited to make self-publishing my primary focus. This venture is a way to satisfy my inner writer and an opportunity to share stories, ideas, and reflections with a broader audience.

Also by MAHESH MATHPAL

www.ingramcontent.com/pod-product-compliance
Lightning Source LLC
Chambersburg PA
CBHW070359230526
45471CB00006B/2645